W9-AOM-116

Table of Contents

Chapter		Page #
1	Goal-Setting Is Writing Down Anything You Want To Become, Do or Have	3
2	You Are Only Qualified For The Goals You Are Willing To Pursue	9
3	Your Goal Will Require A Variety of Relationships	13
4	Your Goal Is Worth Any Investment Necessary To Create The Atmosphere That Keeps You Motivated	17
5	Your Time In The Secret Place Will Expose Any Potential Pitfall In The Pursuit of Your Goals	21
6	You Must Identify Adversarial Relationships That Distract You From Your Goals	25
7	Your Greatest Goal Should Be Knowing God	27

Unless otherwise indicated, all Scripture quotations are taken from the *King James Version* of the Bible.

7 Overlooked Keys To Effective Goal-Setting, Seeds of Wisdom on Goal-Setting, Topic 143
ISBN 1-56394-133-3/B-127
Copyright © 2009 by ***Mike Murdock***
All publishing rights belong exclusively to Wisdom International
Publisher/Editor: Deborah Murdock Johnson
Published by The Wisdom Center · 4051 Denton Hwy. · Ft. Worth, Texas 76117
1-817-759-BOOK · 1-817-759-0300
You Will Love Our Website...! WisdomOnline.com
Printed in the United States of America. All rights reserved under International Copyright Law. Contents and/or cover may not be reproduced in whole or in part in any form without the express written consent of the publisher.

Accuracy Department: To Our Friends and Partners...We welcome any comments on errors or misprints you find in our book...Email our department: AccuracyDept@thewisdomcenter.tv. Your aid in helping us excel is highly valued.

Stop Looking At
Where You Have Been
And Start Looking At
Where You Can Be.

-MIKE MURDOCK

Copyright © 2009 by Mike Murdock • Wisdom International
The Wisdom Center • 4051 Denton Hwy. • Fort Worth, TX 76117

1

Goal-Setting Is Writing Down Anything You Want To Become, Do or Have

You Can Only Do Something You Can See.

You must *see* a goal—before you can *reach* it. You must see it in The World of Your Experience, or The Room of Your Imagination. God explained this phenomenon in Genesis. When the arrogant government leaders decided to build a monument to themselves that would reach the Heavens...God came down to stop it. Yet, He acknowledged the Law of Visualization and its potential. "Now nothing will be restrained from them, which they have imagined to do," (Genesis 11:6).

10 Facts About Setting Goals

1. God Knows Your Desires And Needs. "For your Heavenly Father knoweth that ye have need of all these things," (Matthew 6:32).

2. God Wants Those Dreams And Goals To Happen. "Delight thyself also in the Lord; and He shall give thee the desires of thine heart," (Psalm 37:4).

3. God Expects You To Document Those Desires By Writing Them Down As A Covenant Between You And Him. "Write the vision, and make it plain upon tables, that he may run that readeth it," (Habakkuk 2:2).

4. God Will Impart The Divine Schedule

And Plan For The Achieving of Your Goal. "For the vision is yet for an appointed time, but at the end it shall speak, and not lie: though it tarry, wait for it; because it will surely come, it will not tarry," (Habakkuk 2:3).

5. God Wrote His Own Goals And Dreams Down In The Word. "For I know the thoughts that I think toward you, saith the Lord, thoughts of peace, and not of evil, to give you an expected end," (Jeremiah 29:11).

6. God Plans The Entry of Leaders Years Before Their Birth On The Earth. "Before I formed thee in the belly I knew thee; and before thou camest forth out of the womb I sanctified thee, and I ordained thee a prophet unto the nations," (Jeremiah 1:5).

7. God Even Wrote Down His Commands And Rewards On Tables of Stone For Moses And The Israelites. "And I will write on the tables the words that were in the first tables which thou brakest, and thou shalt put them in the ark," (Deuteronomy 10:2).

8. Uncommon Leaders Know The Power of Writing Down Events, Truths or Covenants For The Purpose of Destiny. "And the Lord said unto Moses, Write this for a memorial in a book, and rehearse it in the ears of Joshua," (Exodus 17:14).

9. Uncommon Prophets Were Instructed To Write Down What Was Worthy of Focus. "Now go, write it before them in a table, and note it in a book, that it may be for the time to come for ever and ever," (Isaiah 30:8).

10. Uncommon Leaders Were Commanded To Write Any Instruction They Received From God. "Thus speaketh the Lord God of Israel, saying, Write thee all the words that I have spoken unto thee in a book," (Jeremiah 30:2).

Take a moment to review the habits of Uncommon Financial Leaders here in our generation. The late Mary Kay Ash, a beautiful business leader, had the remarkable habit of writing down her daily goals—six things she would do that very day. She wrote them down in the order and sequence of their priority or value. Her business was valued at over 1 billion dollars at her death.

3 Goal Sheets

Here are 3 different pages awaiting your personal investment of time, to document your goals...anything you want to become, do or have.

First: ***Your Lifetime Dreams And Goals.***

You may dream of...owning your own business, traveling throughout the world, losing 40 pounds, learning a new language, being debt-free, becoming a missionary. Write it down...in detail.

Second: ***Your 12-Month Goals.***

Anything you want to begin or finish within this next year. It may be to purchase your house, pay your car off, memorize a Scripture a day or lose 20 pounds.

Third: ***Your 30-Day Goals.***

These may include the simple tasks of organizing your mail, cleaning out your closet, returning phone calls, meeting with your financial planner or reading a specific book you have laid to the side.

I read recently that only 3 percent of the United States population have a written list of their dreams and goals. This may explain why 3 percent govern the other 97 percent...3 percent own as much real estate as the remaining 97 percent combined and...the same 3 percent possess as much wealth as the remaining 97 percent *combined.*

Goals matter.

Written goals matter more.

YOUR LIFETIME DREAMS AND GOALS

You may dream of...owning your own business, traveling throughout the world, losing 40 pounds, learning a new language, being debt-free, becoming a missionary. Write it down...in detail.

1. Impart the Wisdom of God
all over the world
2.
3. Counseling Center that
4. will unite family, Heal souls,
and build nations
5.
Release debt of finances,
6. addictions, and etc
7.
Boldness,
8. stronger wisdom of God.
9.
My Children will move and
10. obey in the things of God
11.
Remain forever in the will
12. off God, never worry about being
13. a people pleasers but
God in the name of Jesus
14. pleaser

YOUR 12-MONTH GOALS

Anything you want to begin or finish within this next year. It may be to purchase your house, pay your car off, memorize a Scripture a day or lose 20 pounds. Write it down.

1._____

2._____

3._____

4._____

5._____

6._____

7._____

8._____

9._____

10._____

11._____

12._____

13._____

14._____

YOUR 30-DAY GOALS

These may include the simple tasks of organizing your mail, cleaning out your closet, returning phone calls, meeting with your financial planner or reading a specific book you have laid to the side.

1._____

2._____

3._____

4._____

5._____

6._____

7._____

8._____

9._____

10._____

11._____

12._____

13._____

14._____

2

You Are Only Qualified For The Goals You Are Willing To Pursue

The Proof of Desire Is Pursuit.

You rarely reach for what you really need.

You will always reach for what you desire.

Many were blind during the time of Christ. But, remember the blind man who cried out even louder after being warned by others to be quiet.

Passion pursues.

One woman who had an issue of blood for 12 years pressed through the crowd. Nobody else cared. But, her passion to be healed birthed tenacity, determination and focus. She *received.* (See Matthew 9:20-22.)

God often births Faith-Pictures in your heart. We call them *miracles.* He desires to impart blessings He wants you to possess. But, it is your own personal responsibility to *pursue* for the receiving of those dreams and goals.

God does not respond to *pain.*

God only responds to *pursuit.*

Millions have not grasped this. The whining, complaining and critical unbelieving crowd accuses God continually of not truly caring. You have heard it everywhere..."Why did God let those people die of famine? Why did God permit that tragedy to happen?"

While none of us truly understand all the ways of God, we do know that "No good thing will He withhold from them that walk uprightly," (Psalm 84:11).

Reaching Is The Proof of Humility. The proud withdraw from God. They receive nothing. The humble *reach*...pursue...because they discern God as the True Source of their desired Dream. "For he that cometh to God must believe that He is, and that He is a rewarder of them that diligently seek Him," (Hebrews 11:6).

God Requires Your Pursuit To Even Receive His Forgiveness And Mercy. "Come now, and let us reason together, saith the Lord: though your sins be as scarlet, they shall be as white as snow; though they be red like crimson, they shall be as wool," (Isaiah 1:18).

You Are Not Qualified To Receive From God Until You Ask And Pursue In Faith And Confidence. "But without faith it is impossible to please Him; for he that cometh to God must believe that He is, and that He is a rewarder of them that diligently seek Him," (Hebrews 11:6).

God Always Favors The Aggressive And Persistent. One of the greatest pictures was recorded by Matthew: "And, behold, a woman of Canaan came out of the same coasts, and cried unto Him, saying, Have mercy on me, O Lord, Thou Son of David; my daughter is grievously vexed with a devil. But He answered her not a word. And His disciples came and besought Him, saying, Send her away; for she crieth after us. But He answered and said, I am not sent but unto the lost sheep of the house of Israel. Then came she and worshipped Him, saying, Lord, help me. But He answered and said, It is not meet to take the children's bread, and to cast it to dogs. And she said,

Truth, Lord: yet the dogs eat of the crumbs which fall from their masters' table. Then Jesus answered and said unto her, O woman, great is thy faith: be it unto thee even as thou wilt. And her daughter was made whole from that very hour," (Matthew 15:22-28).

Nobody Else Is Responsible For Motivating or Encouraging You. So, learn to encourage yourself. This was one of the Secrets of David. "Delight thyself also in the Lord; and He shall give thee the desires of thine heart," (Psalm 37:4).

The Holy Spirit documented this quality of David. "And David was greatly distressed;...but David encouraged himself in the Lord," (1 Samuel 30:6).

3 Keys To Developing Your Passion

1. Abandon Any Dream or Goal That No Longer Generates Joy or Energy. It may be a childhood fantasy, or something others thought you should pursue. But, your goals should birth enthusiasm in *you.*

2. Pursue Goals That Qualify For Your Total Focus. Things that truly matter deserve quality hours. Eliminate the part-time interests.

3. Study The Habits of Uncommon Achievers. Thomas Edison said his difference from others was that others thought on many things while he "thought on only one thing all day long."

Jesus focused on His Assignment. "For the Son of man is come to seek and to save that which was lost," (Luke 19:10). Paul wrote, "I press toward the mark for the prize of the high calling of God in Christ Jesus," (Philippians 3:14).

You Are Only Qualified For The Goals You Are Willing To Pursue.

Every Relationship
In Your Life
Will Make A Deposit
or A Withdrawal.

-MIKE MURDOCK

Copyright © 2009 by Mike Murdock • Wisdom International
The Wisdom Center • 4051 Denton Hwy. • Fort Worth, TX 76117

3

Your Goal Will Require A Variety of Relationships

You Cannot Succeed Alone.

The Scriptures teach the necessity of others. "Two are better than one; because they have a good reward for their labour. For if they fall, the one will lift up his fellow: but woe to him that is alone when he falleth; for he hath not another to help him up," (Ecclesiastes 4:9-10).

Jesus did not attempt to reach the world alone. He sent them out two by two. "After these things the Lord appointed other seventy also, and sent them two and two before His face into every city and place, whither He Himself would come," (Luke 10:1).

4 Relationships You Need To Achieve Your Goals

1. You Will Need A Circle of Counsel. "Where no counsel is, the people fall: but in the multitude of counsellers there is safety," (Proverbs 11:14).

Focus Always Creates Blindness.

So, you must have others who see what you cannot see. Every king and world leader selects his personal Circle of Counsel, to increase the quality of his decision-making.

2. You Will Need Uncommon Mentors.

Mentors are not simply teachers—Mentors are *trusted* teachers. Elisha was mentored by Elijah. Timothy was mentored by Paul.

The Quality of The Mentor Determines The Productivity of The Protégé. One way to predict someone's future is to discern who is mentoring them. Your Mentor recognizes your Enemy before you do. Mordecai was aware of Haman before Esther even knew the evil plot herself. "And Mordecai told him of all that had happened unto him, and of the sum of the money that Haman had promised to pay to the king's treasuries for the Jews, to destroy them," (Esther 4:7).

Cheerleaders are wonderful, but coaches win games. *Correction Is As Necessary As Comfort.* Every achiever knows this.

3. You Will Need Intercessors. Queen Esther was a beautiful woman who was the confidante of the king. But, when she focused on the goal of saving her own people she did not rely on her beauty, personality nor even her access to the king. She called a group to fast and pray. "Go, gather together all the Jews that are present in Shushan, and fast ye for me, and neither eat nor drink three days, night or day: I also and my maidens will fast likewise; and so will I go in unto the king, which is not according to the law: and if I perish, I perish," (Esther 4:16).

4. You Will Need Encouragers. That is why the Scriptures instruct us to build up each other. "Brethren, if a man be overtaken in a fault, ye which are spiritual, restore such an one in the spirit of meekness; considering thyself, lest thou also be tempted. Bear ye one another's burdens, and so fulfil the law of Christ," (Galatians 6:1-2).

Your Top 7 Checklist

Take a moment to write down:

1. The Top 7 Names of Those Who Have Consistently Expressed Personal Confidence In You And Your Dreams.

2. The Top 7 Achievers You Know Personally Who Have Achieved Uncommon Goals.

3. The Top 7 Intercessors Who Have A Strong Relationship With The Holy Spirit.

4. The Top 7 Mentors Who Are Qualified To Bring The Gift of Correction Into Your Life.

Are you wise? Are you a fool? It is easy to recognize. The Scriptures reveal the method for discerning the *quality* of your own heart: "Reprove not a scorner, lest he hate thee: rebuke a wise man, and he will love thee," (Proverbs 9:8).

Pursue these relationships. Listen to their counsel. Open your heart up and share the goals that burn within you. You will take giant steps toward your goals when you dare to reach out to involve others.

Your Goal Will Require A Variety of Relationships.

RECOMMENDED INVESTMENTS:

Dream Seeds (Book/B-11/106 pages/$12)
Seeds of Wisdom on Relationships (Book/B-14/32 pages/$3)
Dream Seeds (6 tapes/TS-11/$30)
31 Secrets of The Uncommon Mentor (6 tapes/TS-37/$30)

The Atmosphere
You Create
Determines The Product
You Produce.

-MIKE MURDOCK

Copyright © 2009 by Mike Murdock • Wisdom International
The Wisdom Center • 4051 Denton Hwy. • Fort Worth, TX 76117

4

Your Goal Is Worth Any Investment Necessary To Create The Atmosphere That Keeps You Motivated

Staying Inspired Is Often Your Greatest Battle.

Every dreamer encounters despondency. There are days of great progress and hope. Then, there are seasons of unending frustrations, delays and self-doubts. Some of the great world leaders, such as Winston Churchill and Abraham Lincoln, fought seasons of severe depression. Scriptures are filled with such moments in the lives of powerful spiritual leaders.

Jonah wanted to die after his great revival in Nineveh. "And it came to pass, when the sun did arise, that God prepared a vehement east wind; and the sun beat upon the head of Jonah, that he fainted, and wished in himself to die, and said, It is better for me to die than to live," (Jonah 4:8).

Jesus experienced great heartache. He cried out in the Garden of Gethsemane, "Father, if Thou be willing, remove this cup from Me: nevertheless not My will, but Thine, be done. And there appeared an angel unto Him from Heaven, strengthening Him. And being in an agony He prayed more earnestly: and His sweat was as it were great drops of blood falling down to the ground," (Luke 22:42-44).

Accept such seasons as Moments of Motivation for Pursuing the Mentorship of The Holy Spirit.

1. Anticipate The Erratic Emotional Waves That Dash Against You. It is normal for those pursuing worthy and uncommon goals.

2. Identify Your Personal Sources of Enthusiasm. You may require a specific type of music. Identify it. I like waterfalls, candles and soft music. I require a peaceful climate. Others may need a loud, boisterous atmosphere to unlock their passion and enthusiasm. Invest the time necessary to think this through for yourself and your specific or changing needs.

3. Invest In Any Equipment, Furnishings, Clothing or Tools That Will Sculpture The Atmosphere That Feeds Your Enthusiasm And Passion. A few days ago, I explained this to a young protégé. He was puzzled by my purchasing a new laptop. "But, you already have a very nice laptop," he said.

"Son, the new one contains the full wireless capabilities inside, contains a second back-up battery and has double the memory for all my Wisdom Files. It has the newest programs, the infrared, the serial and USB ports," I explained.

His goal was to save *money.*

My goal was to save *time.*

His goal was to *accumulate.*

My goal was to *accomplish.*

My enthusiasm, energy and passion is worth far more than $3,500. So, I was willing to invest whatever it takes to feed my joy...my energy...because money is far easier to replace than motivation and passion.

Lost money can be regained...when you are *motivated.*

If you lose motivation, you lose *everything.*

I do not like cheap candles that burn without a strong fragrance. I invest in candles that fill up the room with a Heavenly aroma!

The atmosphere is worth the cost.

My goal is worth the investment.

Nobody else can do this for you. So, invest whatever is necessary to protect your focus and create the climate that keeps you continually inspired and energized.

Your Goal Is Worth Any Investment Necessary To Create The Atmosphere That Keeps You Motivated.

Where You Are
Determines
What Grows In You.

-MIKE MURDOCK

Copyright © 2009 by Mike Murdock • Wisdom International
The Wisdom Center • 4051 Denton Hwy. • Fort Worth, TX 76117

5

Your Time In The Secret Place Will Expose Any Potential Pitfall In The Pursuit of Your Goals

Every Pitfall Is Avoidable.

You can eliminate ten thousand heartaches and tears by listening to the Voice of The Spirit. The cry of Jesus was to "...hear what the Spirit saith," (see Revelation 3:22).

The Role of The Holy Spirit Is To Protect You. That was evident when The Holy Spirit used Agabus to warn of approaching catastrophe. "And there stood up one of them named Agabus, and signified by the Spirit that there should be great dearth throughout all the world: which came to pass in the days of Claudius Caesar," (Acts 11:28).

The Holy Spirit Discerns The Hidden Motives And Unspoken Agendas of Others. Deception is deadly.

One Person in your life can create 20 years of tears.

One Trap can destroy a thousand dreams God desires for you.

One Lie can devastate the most noble goal and dream.

Time with The Holy Spirit is the *greatest*

investment of your life. "Likewise the Spirit also helpeth our infirmities: for we know not what we should pray for as we ought: but the Spirit (Himself) maketh intercession for us with groanings which cannot be uttered," (Romans 8:26).

The Holy Spirit Anticipates The Adversarial Atmosphere You Will Enter Today. The ungodly reign...for the present. Traps are set. Poisonous arrows are in the bows of your enemies. You need a Defense. The most qualified Defense is the Master Mentor who provides The Wisdom of The Word...He will become an Enemy to your enemies! "...and vexed His holy Spirit: therefore He was turned to be their enemy, and He fought against them," (Isaiah 63:10).

The most memorable day of my life was Wednesday, July 13, 1994...the day I fell in love with The Holy Spirit. He radically changed my life...my focus...my plans. He became my Obsession, The Love of my life. I would trade every discovery of my life for what I have discovered about Him. He is The Comforter, The Spirit of Wisdom and The One Who Stayed. "And I will pray the Father, and He shall give you another Comforter, that He may abide with you for ever," (John 14:16).

- ▶ You must *know* Him—not merely experience Him.
- ▶ You must *sit* at His feet—not merely touch Him.
- ▶ You must establish The Secret Place...a private Room of Solitude where you meet with Him daily.

1. Enter The Secret Place Singing To Him. (See Psalm 100:2.) Love Him. Worship Him. Bishop David Oyedepo spoke this to me while I was having lunch in his home in Lagos, Nigeria. "Gratitude provokes joy. Joy provokes praise. Your praise creates Divine Presence."

2. Enter The Same Time Each Morning. Habit is a gift from God. Habit takes you further than desire. It is your appointment with The Spirit of Wisdom.

3. Stay In His Presence Long Enough To Create A Memory. The prodigal son lost finances, friends, favor and influence...but, satan could not steal his memories.

4. Keep A Daily Wisdom Journal. Document His Master Secrets to you. Your success matters to Him.

Your Time In The Secret Place Will Expose Any Potential Pitfall In The Pursuit of Your Goals.

RECOMMENDED INVESTMENTS:
The Holy Spirit Handbook, Vol. 1 (Book/B-100/153 pages/$15)
Where Miracles Are Born (Book/B-115/32 pages/$7)
The Greatest Day of My Life (Book/B-116/32 pages/$7)

Anything Good Is
Hated By
Everything Evil.

-MIKE MURDOCK

Copyright © 2009 by Mike Murdock • Wisdom International
The Wisdom Center • 4051 Denton Hwy. • Fort Worth, TX 76117

6

You Must Identify Adversarial Relationships That Distract You From Your Goals

You Will Always Have An Enemy.

Jesus had enemies and the servant is not above his lord. He instructed us to expect adversaries. "Blessed are ye, when men shall hate you, and when they shall separate you from their company, and shall reproach you, and cast out your name as evil, for the Son of man's sake," (Luke 6:22).

5 Ways To Identify An Enemy To Your Goals

1. An Enemy Is Anyone Who Weakens Your Influence With Others. Nehemiah faced this. Ezra experienced it also. "Hired counsellors against them, to frustrate their purpose," (Ezra 4:5).

2. An Enemy Is Anyone Who Focuses On Your Past Instead of Your Future. "Remember ye not the former things, neither consider the things of old. Behold, I will do a new thing; now it shall spring forth; shall ye not know it? I will even make a way in the wilderness, and rivers in the desert," (Isaiah 43:18-19).

3. An Enemy Is Anyone Who Attempts To Weaken Your Passion Through Contempt or

Criticism. Nehemiah experienced this from Tobiah who sneered at the quality of the walls being rebuilt. "Now Tobiah the Ammonite was by him, and he said, Even that which they build, if a fox go up, he shall even break down their stone wall," (Nehemiah 4:3).

4. An Enemy Is Anyone Who Thinks You Are Unworthy of Achieving A God-Given Goal. Jesus experienced this continually from those who felt nothing good could come from Nazareth. "Is not this the carpenter, the son of Mary, the brother of James, and Joses, and of Juda, and Simon? and are not His sisters here with us? And they were offended at Him," (Mark 6:3).

5. Your Enemy Is Anyone Who Knowingly Distracts You From Your Goal. Distraction Is Always The Goal of An Adversary.

Remember this, The Only Reason Men Fail Is...*Broken Focus.* Discern this. Move swiftly to protect your focus.

Special Reminders...

▶ *Your Enemy May Exist In Your Own Home.*

Jesus warned us of this possibility. "And a man's foes shall be they of his own household," (Matthew 10:36).

▶ *Fatigue Is An Enemy To Your Goal.*

Tired eyes never see a great future. God rested... on the seventh day. Jesus commanded His disciples to come apart from the crowds and the activities pressing them. "And He said unto them, Come ye yourselves apart into a desert place, and rest a while: for there were many coming and going, and they had no leisure so much as to eat," (Mark 6:31).

I highly recommend my book, *The Law of Recognition.* It contains a chapter listing "92 Facts You Should Know About Enemies."

You Must Identify Adversarial Relationships That Distract You From Your Goals.

7

Your Greatest Goal Should Be Knowing God

The Goals of God Are More Important Than Your's.

God has a Master Plan for your success. Nobody cares more about your goals and dreams than The Creator Who has birthed them within you. But, you must never allow them to become a substitute for Him. Like Abraham, your loyalty and affection will be tested. (See Genesis 22:8-14.)

God Is A Jealous God Who Will Not Tolerate The Worship of Anything Else In Your Life. "For thou shalt worship no other god: for the Lord, Whose name is Jealous, is a jealous God: Lest thou make a covenant with the inhabitants of the land, and they go a whoring after their gods, and do sacrifice unto their gods, and one call thee, and thou eat of his sacrifice," (Exodus 34:14-15).

God Is Greatly Concerned That Obedience Becomes Your Focus, Instead of His Blessings. "Then thine heart be lifted up, and thou forget the Lord thy God, which brought thee forth out of the land of Egypt, from the house of bondage; And it shall be, if thou do at all forget the Lord thy God, and walk after other gods, and serve them, and worship them, I testify against you this day that ye shall surely perish," (Deuteronomy 8:14, 19).

Your Obedience Includes A Church Home Where

You Receive Spiritual Mentorship. "Not forsaking the assembling of ourselves together, as the manner of some is; but exhorting one another: and so much the more, as ye see the day approaching," (Hebrews 10:25).

I am the son of a pastor. My father often warned his people to put God first in everything. He saw parents obsessed with their children's involvement with school sports...and eventually stop coming to the Wednesday night services. He saw businesses flourish and their owners too busy to come to Sunday night services. *Anything That Takes You Away From His Presence Is A Trap.* Do not fall for it.

Many who prosper financially have failed miserably in their prayer life as their business became their "god."

Many who received the gift of children from God made their children their "god" and put sports and vacations ahead of their spiritual mentorship. The loss is deadly.

- ▶ Stay involved with your church.
- ▶ Respect the correction of your Shepherd and Pastor.
- ▶ Mentor your family in The Word of God.
- ▶ Keep your morning appointments with The Holy Spirit.
- ▶ Keep your word to others whatever the cost.
- ▶ Fight to maintain your integrity.

When you do, God will commit Himself to you and His success plans for you...will surely come to pass at the appointed time. "For I know the thoughts that I think toward you, saith the Lord, thoughts of peace, and not of evil, to give you an expected end. Then shall ye call upon Me, and ye shall go and pray unto Me, and I will hearken unto you. And ye shall seek Me, and find Me, when ye shall search for Me with all your heart," (Jeremiah 29:11-13).

Your Greatest Goal Should Be Knowing God.

My Closing Thought

If this Wisdom book has blessed you, I'd love to hear from you! You may order additional copies for a friend, cell group or associates at your workplace.

The Greatest Gift of All...Is The Gift of Wisdom.

Quantity Price List For
7 Overlooked Keys To Effective Goal-Setting (B-127)

Quantity		Cost each	Discount	Quantity		Cost each	Discount
1-9	=	$5.00 ea.	Retail	2000-4999	=	$2.00 ea.	60%
10-499	=	$3.00 ea.	40%	5000-up	=	Contact Office	
500-1999	=	$2.50 ea.	50%				

(Add 20% shipping all single titles.)

Recommended For Your Wisdom Library:

The Assignment Vol. 1: The Dream & The Destiny (Book/B-74/164 pages/$12)

The Assignment Vol. 2: The Anointing & The Adversity (Book/B-75/192 pages/$12)

The Assignment Vol. 3: The Trials & The Triumphs (Book/B-97/160 pages/$12)

The Assignment Vol. 4: The Pain & The Passion (Book/B-98/144 pages/$12)

The Leadership Secrets of Jesus (Book/B-91/196 pages/$12)

The Law of Recognition (Book/B-114/247 pages/$15)

Wisdom for Winning (Book/B-01/228 pages/$10)

The Assignment (6 Tapes/TS-52/$30)

The Wisdom Center
4051 Denton Hwy.
Fort Worth, TX 76117
817-759-BOOK
817-759-0300
You Will Love Our Website...!
WisdomOnline.com

Dear Friend,

You matter.

You are important to God. If you need special prayer, do not hesitate to write today.

My staff and I will pray for you. I will write you back.

God has brought us together for a reason.

Will you become my Monthly Faith Partner?

Your Seeds of Loving Support will bless so many...and birth uncommon increase in your own life.

When you sow, expect 4 Scriptural Harvests:

- Uncommon Protection (Mal. 3:10-11)
- Uncommon Favor (Lk. 6:38)
- Uncommon Health (Isa. 58:8)
- Uncommon Financial Ideas (Deut. 8:18)

An Uncommon Seed Always Creates An Uncommon Harvest (Mk. 10:28-30).

Looking For Your Letter,

Mike Murdock

Miracle 7 BOOK PAK!

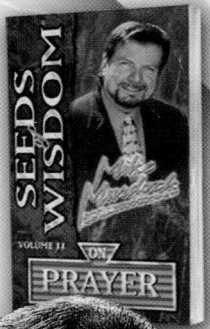

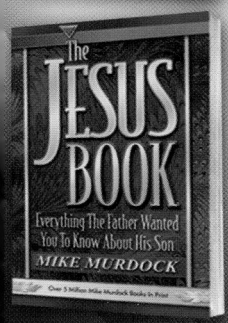

DR. MIKE MURDOCK

1. **Dream Seeds** (Book/B-11/106pg/$12)
2. **7 Hidden Keys to Favor** (Book/B-119/32pg/$7)
3. **Seeds of Wisdom on Miracles** (Book/B-15/32pg/$
4. **Seeds of Wisdom on Prayer** (Book/B-23/32pg/$3)
5. **The Jesus Book** (Book/B-27/166pg/$10)
6. **The Memory Bible on Miracles** (Book/B-208/32pg/$3)
7. **The Mentor's Manna on Attitude** (Book/B-58/32pg/$3)

D0123792

om Is The Principal

Add 20% For S/H

Quantity Prices Available Upon Request

*Each Wisdom Book may be purchased separately if so desired.

THE WISDOM CENTER
4051 Denton Highway • Fort Worth, TX 76117
1-817-759-BOOK
1-817-759-0300
You Will Love Our Website...!
WISDOMONLINE.COM

A

Crisis 7 BOOK PAK!

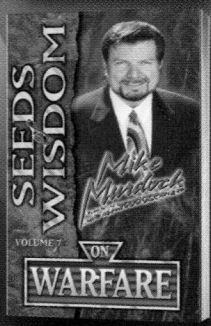

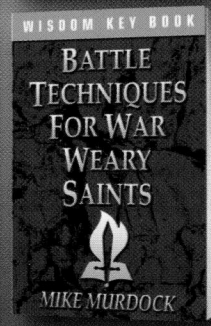

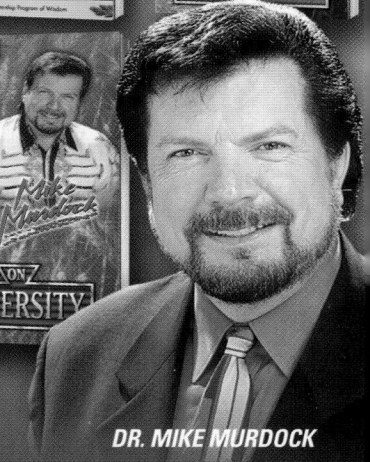

DR. MIKE MURDOCK

1. **The Survival Bible** (Book/B-29/248pg/$10)
2. **Wisdom For Crisis Times** (Book/B-40/112pg/$9)
3. **Seeds of Wisdom on Motivating Yourself** (Book/B-171/32pg/$5)
4. **Seeds of Wisdom on Overcoming** (Book/B-17/32pg/$3)
5. **Seeds of Wisdom on Warfare** (Book/B-19/32pg/$3)
6. **Battle Techniques For War Weary Saints** (Book/B-07/32pg/$5)
7. **Seeds of Wisdom on Adversity** (Book/B-21/32pg/$3)

The Wisdom Center
Crisis 7 Book Pak!
Only $30 ~~$38~~ Value
WBL-25
Wisdom Is The Principal Thing

Add 20% For S/H

Quantity Prices Available Upon Request

*Each Wisdom Book may be purchased separately if so desired.

B

THE WISDOM CENTER
4051 Denton Highway • Fort Worth, TX 76117

1-817-759-BOOK
1-817-759-0300

You Will Love Our Website...!
WISDOMONLINE.COM

Money 7 BOOK PAK!

DR. MIKE MURDOCK

1. **Secrets of the Richest Man Who Ever Lived** (Book/B-99/179pg/$12)
2. **The Blessing Bible** (Book/B-28/252pg/$10)
3. **Born To Taste The Grapes** (Book/B-65/32pg/$3)
4. **Creating Tomorrow Through Seed-Faith** (Book/B-06/32pg/$5)
5. **Seeds of Wisdom on Prosperity** (Book/B-22/32pg/$5)
6. **Seven Obstacles To Abundant Success** (Book/B-64/32pg/$5)
7. **Ten Lies Many People Believe About Money** (Book/B-04/32pg/$5)

The Wisdom Center
Money 7 Book Pak!
Only **$30** ~~$45~~ Value
WBL-30
Wisdom Is The Principal Thing

Add 20% For S/H

Each Wisdom Book may be purchased separately if so desired.

THE WISDOM CENTER
4051 Denton Highway • Fort Worth, TX 76117

1-817-759-BOOK
1-817-759-0300

You Will Love Our Website...!
WISDOMONLINE.COM

C

Career 7

Book Pak For Business People!

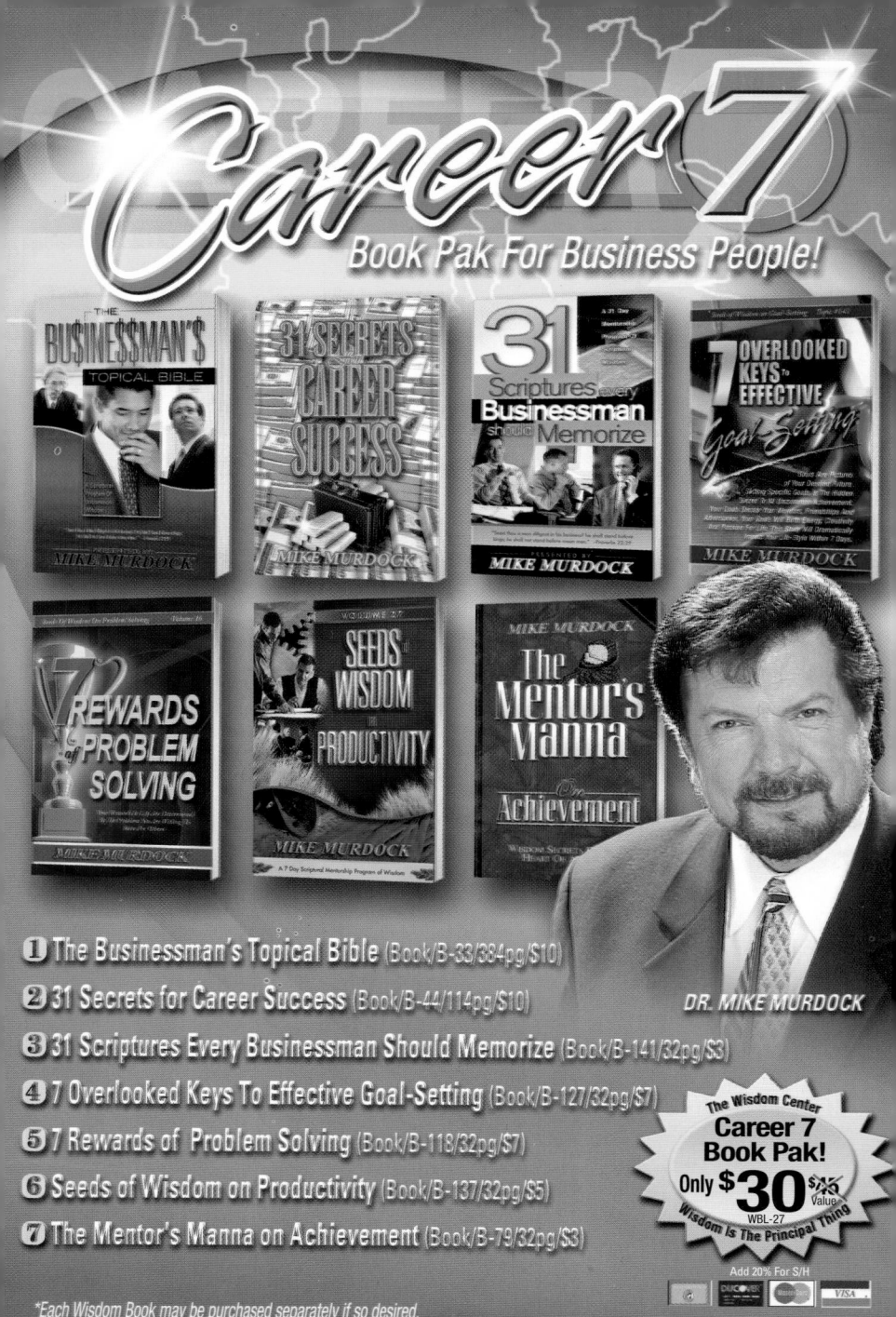

DR. MIKE MURDOCK

1. The Businessman's Topical Bible (Book/B-33/384pg/$10)
2. 31 Secrets for Career Success (Book/B-44/114pg/$10)
3. 31 Scriptures Every Businessman Should Memorize (Book/B-141/32pg/$3)
4. 7 Overlooked Keys To Effective Goal-Setting (Book/B-127/32pg/$7)
5. 7 Rewards of Problem Solving (Book/B-118/32pg/$7)
6. Seeds of Wisdom on Productivity (Book/B-137/32pg/$5)
7. The Mentor's Manna on Achievement (Book/B-79/32pg/$3)

The Wisdom Center
Career 7 Book Pak!
Only $30 $35 Value
WBL-27
Wisdom Is The Principal Thing

Add 20% For S/H

*Each Wisdom Book may be purchased separately if so desired.

D

THE WISDOM CENTER
4051 Denton Highway • Fort Worth, TX 76117

1-817-759-BOOK
1-817-759-0300

You Will Love Our Website...!
WISDOMONLINE.COM

101 Wisdom Keys That Have Most Changed My Life.

SERIES 2
The SCHOOL of WISDOM
101 WISDOM KEYS THAT HAVE MOST CHANGED MY LIFE
MIKE MURDOCK

THE LAWS OF LIFE SERIES
The Law of Recognition
Discovering the Gifts, Opportunities, & Relationships That God Has Already Placed In Your Life
MIKE MURDOCK

TS-42

School of Wisdom #2 Pak!

- What Attracts Others Toward You
- The Secret of Multiplying Your Financial Blessings
- What Stops The Flow of Your Faith
- Why Some Fail And Others Succeed
- How To Discern Your Life Assignment
- How To Create Currents of Favor With Others
- How To Defeat Loneliness
- 47 Keys In Recognizing The Mate God Has Approved For You
- 14 Facts You Should Know About Your Gifts And Talents
- 17 Important Facts You Should Remember About Your Weakness
- And Much, Much More...

The Wisdom Center
School of Wisdom #2 Pak!
Only $30 $45 Value
PAK002
Wisdom Is The Principal Thing

Add 20% For S/H

THE WISDOM CENTER
4051 Denton Highway • Fort Worth, TX 76117
1-817-759-BOOK
1-817-759-0300
You Will Love Our Website...!
WISDOMONLINE.COM
E

The Businessman's Devotion
Book Pak!

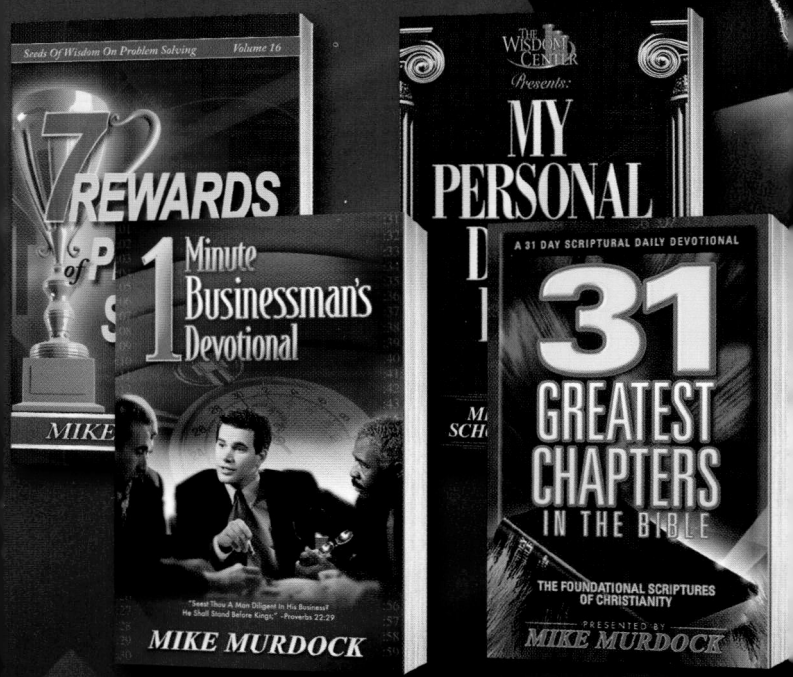

1. **7 Rewards of Problem Solving** (Book/B-118/32pg/$7)
2. **My Personal Dream Book** (Book/B-143/32pg/$5)
3. **1 Minute Businessman's Devotional** (Book/B-42/224pg/$12)
4. **31 Greatest Chapters In The Bible** (Book/B-54/138pg/$10)

The Wisdo
Th
Busines
Devotional 4
Only $2
PAK
Wisdom Is The

Add 20%

THE WISDOM CENTER
4051 Denton Highway • Fort Worth, TX 76117
1-817-759-BOOK
1-817-759-0300

You Will Love Our
WISDOMONLI

Millionaire-Talk

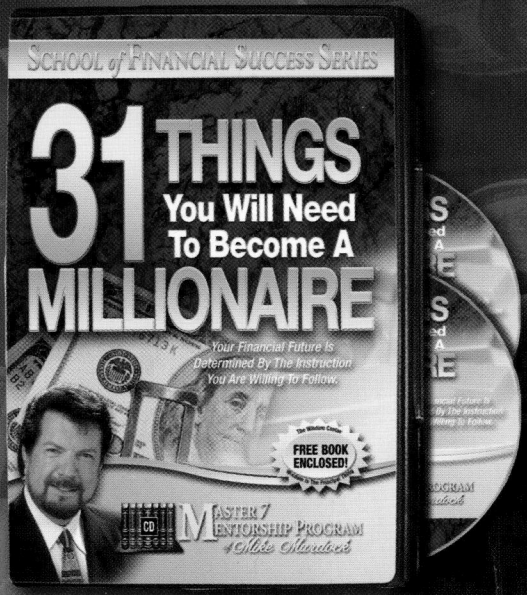

DR. MIKE MURDOCK

MY GIFT OF APPRECIATION
GIFT of Appreciation
Wisdom Is The Principal Thing

31 Things You Will Need To Become A Millionaire (2-CD's/WCPL-116)

Topics Include:

- ***You Will Need Financial Heroes***
- ***Your Willingness To Negotiate Everything***
- ***You Must Have The Ability To Transfer Your Enthusiasm, Your Vision To Others***
- ***Know Your Competition***
- ***Be Willing To Train Your Team Personally As To Your Expectations***
- ***Hire Professionals To Do A Professional's Job***

I have asked the Lord for 3,000 special partners who will sow an extra Seed of $58 towards our Television Outreach Ministry. Your Seed is so appreciated! Remember to request your Gift CD's, 2 Disc Volume, ***31 Things You Will Need To Become A Millionaire,*** when you write this week!

THE WISDOM CENTER
4051 Denton Highway • Fort Worth, TX 76117
1-817-759-BOOK
1-817-759-0300
You Will Love Our Website...!
WISDOMONLINE.COM

G

The CRISIS COLLECTION

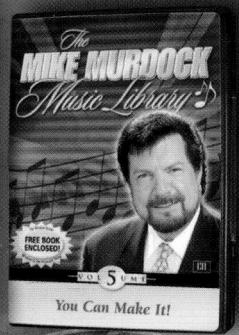

You Get All 6 For One Great Price!

1. **7 Keys For Surviving A Crisis** (DVD/MMPL-04D/$10)
2. **You Can Make It!** (Music CD/MMML-05/$10)
3. **Wisdom For Crisis Times** (6 Cassettes/TS-40/$30)
4. **Seeds of Wisdom on Overcoming** (Book/B-17/32pg/$3)
5. **Seeds of Wisdom on Motivating Yourself** (Book/B-171/32pg/$5)
6. **Wisdom For Crisis Times** (Book/B-40/112pg/$9)

Also Included... Two Free Bonus Books!

**Each Wisdom Product may be purchased separately if so desired.*

The Wisdom Center
The Crisis Collection
Only $40 $87 Value
PAK-16
Wisdom Is The Principal Thing

Add 20% For S/H

H

THE WISDOM CENTER
4051 Denton Highway • Fort Worth, TX 76117

1-817-759-BOOK
1-817-759-0300

You Will Love Our Website...!
WISDOMONLINE.COM

THE TURNAROUND Collection

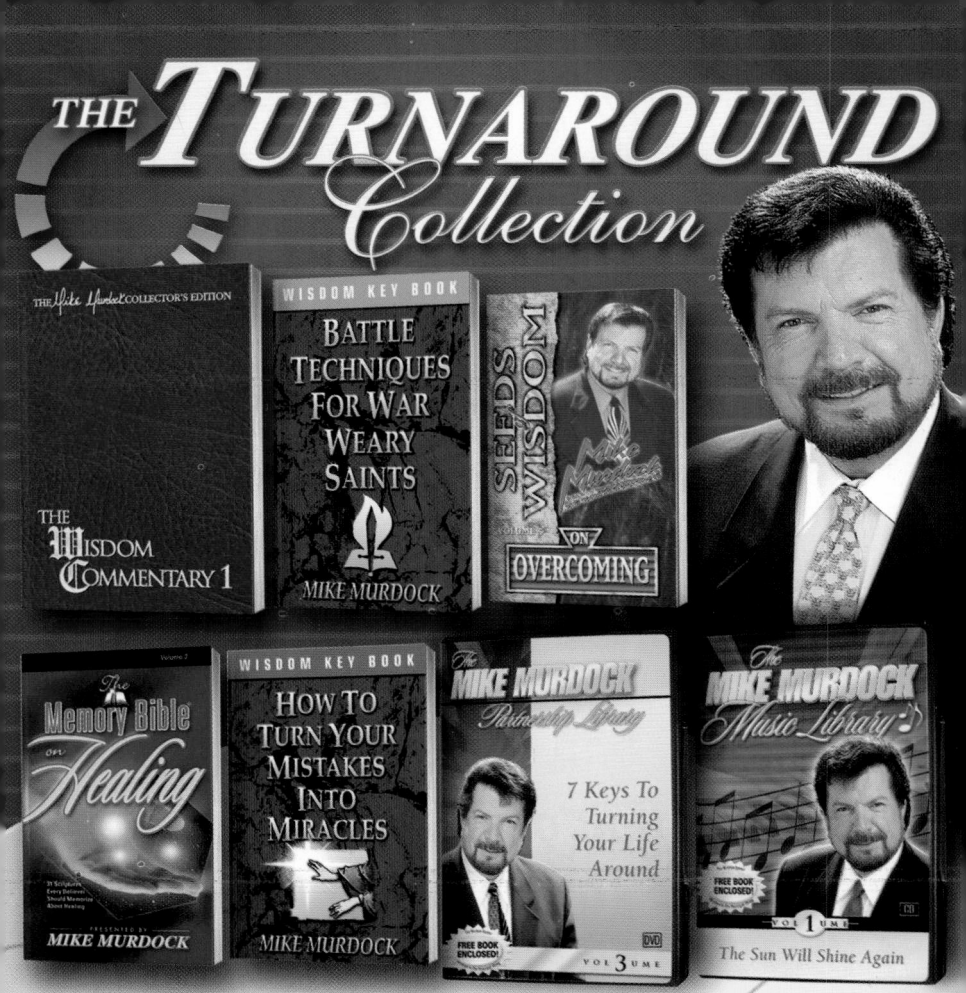

1. **The Wisdom Commentary Vol. 1** (Book/B-136/256pg/52 Topics/$25)
2. **Battle Techniques For War Weary Saints** (Book/B-07/32pg/$5)
3. **Seeds of Wisdom on Overcoming** (Book/B-17/32pg/$3)
4. **The Memory Bible on Healing** (Book/B-196/32pg/$5)
5. **How To Turn Your Mistakes Into Miracles** (Book/B-56/32pg/$5)
6. **7 Keys To Turning Your Life Around** (DVD/MMPL-03D/$10)
7. **The Sun Will Shine Again** (Music CD/MMML-01/$10)

The Wisdom Center
The Turnaround Collection
Only $40 ~~$53~~ Value
PAK-15
Wisdom Is The Principal Thing

Add 20% For S/H

*Each Wisdom Product may be purchased separately if so desired.

THE WISDOM CENTER
4051 Denton Highway • Fort Worth, TX 76117
1-817-759-BOOK
1-817-759-0300
You Will Love Our Website...!
WISDOMONLINE.COM

Favor 4!

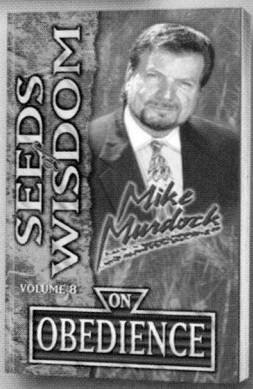

This Collection of Wisdom Will Change The Seasons of Your Life Forever!

1. **The School of Wisdom #4 / 31 Keys To Unleashing Uncommon Favor...Tape Series** (6 Cassettes/TS-44/$30)
2. **The Hidden Power of Right Words...** Master 7 Mentorship Program of Mike Murdock (CD/WCPL-27/$10)
3. **7 Hidden Keys to Favor** (Book/B-119/32pg/$7)
4. **Seeds of Wisdom on Obedience** (Book/B-20/32pg/$5)

The Wisdom Center
Favor 4 Collection!
Only $35 $52 Value
PAK-12
Wisdom Is The Principal Thing

Add 20% For S/H

*Each Wisdom Product may be purchased separately if so desired.

J THE WISDOM CENTER 4051 Denton Highway • Fort Worth, TX 76117
THE WISDOM CENTER 1-817-759-BOOK 1-817-759-0300
You Will Love Our Website...! **WISDOMONLINE.COM**

Financial $ecrets.

Your Financial World Will Change Forever.

Video 2-Pak!

- 8 Scriptural Reasons You Should Pursue Financial Prosperity
- The Secret Prayer Key You Need When Making A Financial Request To God
- The Weapon of Expectation And The 5 Miracles It Unlocks
- How To Discern Those Who Qualify To Receive Your Financial Assistance
- How To Predict The Miracle Moment God Will Schedule Your Financial Breakthrough
- Habits of Uncommon Achievers
- The Greatest Success Law I Ever Discovered
- How To Discern Your Place of Assignment, The Only Place Financial Provision Is Guaranteed
- 3 Secret Keys In Solving Problems For Others

The Wisdom Center
Video 2-Pak!
Only $30 ~~$60~~ Value
VIPAK-01
Wisdom Is The Principal Thing

Add 20% For S/H

*Each Wisdom Product may be purchased separately if so desired.

THE WISDOM CENTER 4051 Denton Highway • Fort Worth, TX 76117
1-817-759-BOOK
1-817-759-0300
You Will Love Our Website...!
WISDOMONLINE.COM
K

THE WISDOM BIBLE

Partnership Editio

Over 120 Wisdom Study Guides Included Such As:

- *10 Qualities of Uncommon Achievers*
- *18 Facts You Should Know About The Anointing*
- *21 Facts To Help You Identify Those Assigned To You*
- *31 Facts You Should Know About Your Assignment*
- *8 Keys That Unlock Victory In Every Attack*
- *22 Defense Techniques To Remember During Seasons of Personal Attack*
- *20 Wisdom Keys And Techniques To Remember During An Uncommon Battle*
- *11 Benefits You Can Expect From God*
- *31 Facts You Should Know About Favor*
- *The Covenant of 58 Blessings*
- *7 Keys To Receiving Your Miracle*
- *16 Facts You Should Remember About Contentious People*
- *5 Facts Solomon Taught About Contracts*
- *7 Facts You Should Know About Conflict*
- *6 Steps That Can Unlock Your Self-Confidence*
- *And Much More!*

Your Partnership makes such a difference in The Wisdom Center Outreach Ministries. I wanted to place a Gift in your hand that could last a lifetime for you and your family...**The Wisdom Study Bible.**

40 Years of Personal Notes...this Partnership Edition Bible contains 160 pages of my Personal Study Notes...that could forever change your Bible Study of The Word of God. This **Partnership Edition...**is my personal **Gift of Appreciation** when you sow your Sponsorship Seed of $1,000 to help us complete The Prayer Center and TV Studio Complex. An Uncommon Seed Always Creates An Uncommon Harvest!

Mike

Thank you from my heart for your Seed of Obedience (Luke 6:38).

L

THE WISDOM CENTER
4051 Denton Highway • Fort Worth, TX 76117

1-817-759-BOOK
1-817-759-0300

You Will Love Our Website...!
WISDOMONLINE.COM

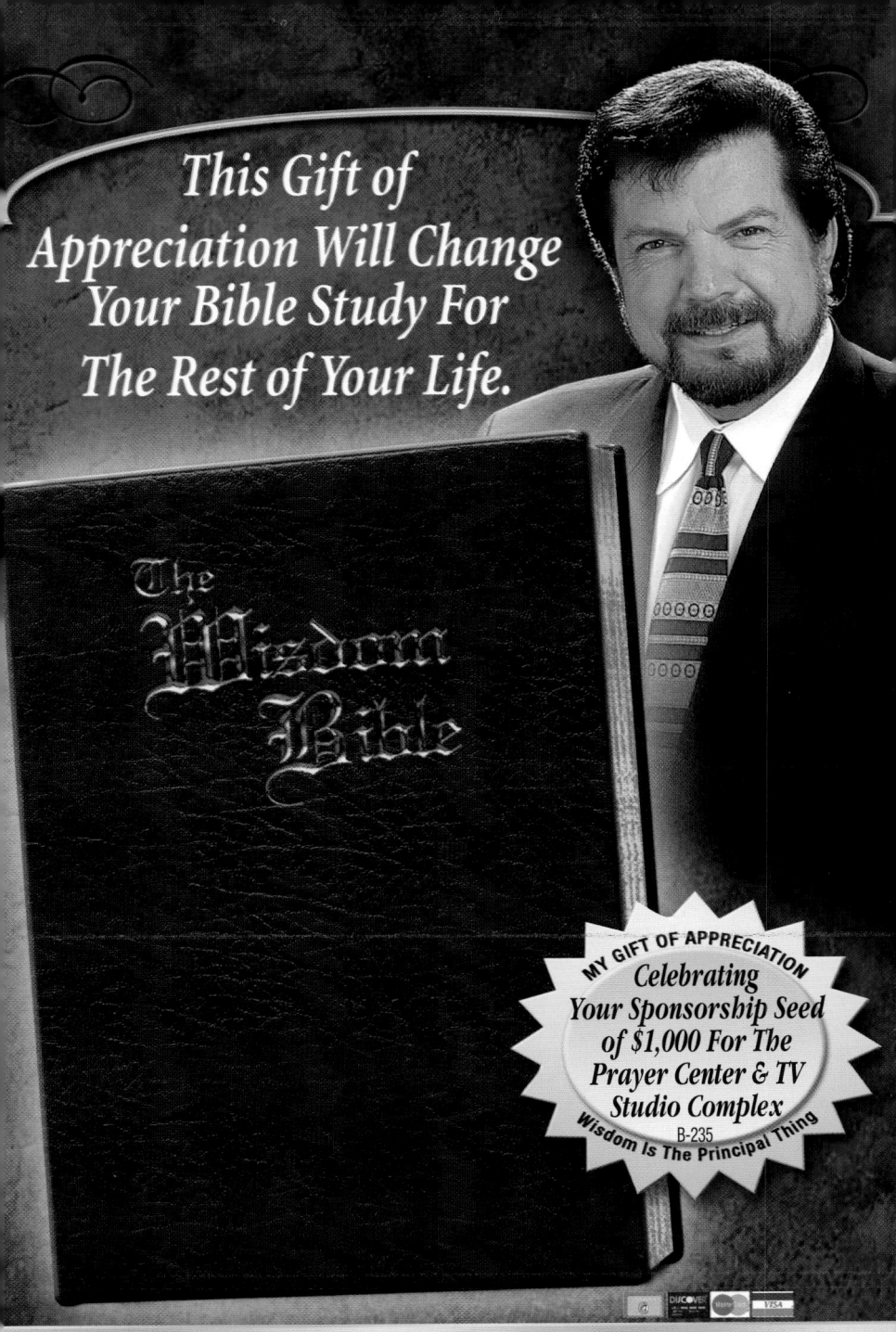
This Gift of Appreciation Will Change Your Bible Study For The Rest of Your Life.
The Wisdom Bible
MY GIFT OF APPRECIATION
Celebrating Your Sponsorship Seed of $1,000 For The Prayer Center & TV Studio Complex
B-235
Wisdom Is The Principal Thing
THE WISDOM CENTER
4051 Denton Highway • Fort Worth, TX 76117
1-817-759-BOOK
1-817-759-0300
You Will Love Our Website...!
WISDOMONLINE.COM
M

Spirit Music.

TS-59

The Wisdom Center
Free Book ENCLOSED!
B-100 ($15 Value)
Wisdom Is The Principal Thing

Songs...

1. A Holy Place
2. Anything You Want
3. Everything Comes From You
4. Fill This Place With Your Presence
5. First Thing Every Morning
6. Holy Spirit, I Want To Hear You
7. Holy Spirit, Move Again
8. Holy Spirit, You Are Enough
9. I Don't Know What I Would Do Without You
10. I Let Go (of Anything That Stops Me)
11. I'll Just Fall On You
12. I Love You, Holy Spirit
13. I'm Building My Life Around You
14. I'm Giving Myself To You
15. I'm In Love! I'm In Love!
16. I Need Water (Holy Spirit, You're My Well)
17. In The Secret Place
18. In Your Presence, I'm Always Changed
19. In Your Presence (Miracles Are Born)
20. I've Got To Live In Your Presence
21. I Want To Hear Your Voice
22. I Will Do Things Your Way
23. Just One Day At A Time
24. Meet Me In The Secret Place
25. More Than Ever Before
26. Nobody Else Does What You Do
27. No No Walls!
28. Nothing Else Matters Anymore (Since I've Been In The Presence of You Lord)
29. Nowhere Else
30. Once Again You've Answered
31. Only A Fool Would Try (To Live Without You)
32. Take Me Now
33. Teach Me How To Please You
34. There's No Place I'd Rather Be
35. Thy Word Is All That Matters
36. When I Get In Your Presence
37. You're The Best Thing (That's Ever Happened To Me)
38. You Are Wonderful
39. You've Done It Once
40. You Keep Changing Me
41. You Satisfy

The Wisdom Center
6 Tapes/Only $30*
PAK007
Wisdom Is The Principal Thing

Add 20% For S/H

N

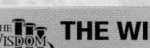

THE WISDOM CENTER
4051 Denton Highway • Fort Worth, TX 76117

1-817-759-BOOK
1-817-759-0300

You Will Love Our Website...!
WISDOMONLINE.COM

YOUR ASSIGNMENT IS YOUR DISTINCTION FROM OTHERS.

Assignment 4 Book Pak!

Uncommon Wisdom For Discovering Your Life Assignment.

1 The Dream & The Destiny
Vol 1 (Book/B-74/164 pg/$12)

2 The Anointing & The Adversity
Vol 2 (Book/B-75/192 pg/$12)

3 The Trials & The Triumphs
Vol 3 (Book/B-97/160 pg/$12)

4 The Pain & The Passion
Vol 4 (Book/B-98/144 pg/$12)

The Wisdom Center
Assignment 4 Book Pak!
Only $30 ~~$48~~ Value
WBL-14
Wisdom Is The Principal Thing

Add 20% For S/H04

*Each Wisdom Book may be purchased separately if so desired.

THE WISDOM CENTER
4051 Denton Highway • Fort Worth, TX 76117
1-817-759-BOOK
1-817-759-0300
You Will Love Our Website...!
WISDOMONLINE.COM

JOIN THE

Wisdom Key 3000 TODAY!

Will You Become My Ministry Partner In The Work of God?

Dear Friend,

God has connected us!

I have asked The Holy Spirit for 3000 Special Partners who will plant a monthly Seed of $58.00 to help me bring the gospel around the world. (58 represents 58 kinds of blessings in the Bible.)

Will you become my monthly Faith Partner in The Wisdom Key 3000? Your monthly Seed of $58.00 is so powerful in helping heal broken lives. When you sow into the work of God, 4 Miracle Harvests are guaranteed in Scripture, Isaiah 58...

- Uncommon Health (Isaiah 58)
- Uncommon Wisdom For Decision-Making (Isaiah 58)
- Uncommon Financial Favor (Isaiah 58)
- Uncommon Family Restoration (Isaiah 58)

Your Faith Partner,

Mike Murdock

P.S. Please clip the coupon attached and return it to me today, so I can rush the Wisdom Key Partnership Pak to you...or call me at 1-817-759-0300. PP-03

☐ ***Yes Mike, I want to join The Wisdom Key 3000. Please rush The Wisdom Key Partnership Pak to me today!***

☐ ***Enclosed is my first monthly Seed-Faith Promise of:***

☐ ***$58*** ☐ ***Other $_____.***

☐CHECK ☐MONEY ORDER ☐AMEX ☐DISCOVER ☐MASTERCARD ☐VISA

Credit Card # _____ Exp. ____/____

Signature _____

Name _____ Birth Date ____/____

Address _____

City _____ State _____ Zip _____

Phone _____ E-Mail _____

Your Seed-Faith Offerings are used to support The Wisdom Center, and all of its programs. The Wisdom Center reserves the right to redirect funds as needed in order to carry out our charitable purpose. In the event The Wisdom Center receives more funds for the project than needed, the excess will be used for another worthy outreach. (Your transactions may be electronically deposited.)

THE WISDOM CENTER
4051 Denton Highway • Fort Worth, TX 76117
1-817-759-BOOK
1-817-759-2665
1-817-759-0300
You Will Love Our Website...!
WisdomOnline.com

Available Now... Online!

7 Master Keys To Organizing Your World And Simplifying Your Life (CD /WCPL-150/$10)

Trustworthiness
(CD /WCPL-282/$10)

Go Online And Order Your Copy Today...! WisdomOnline.com

© 2008. Wisdom International. All Rights Reserved. Unauthorized Duplication Is A Violation Of Applicable Laws.

DR. MIKE MURDOCK is in tremendous demand as one of the most dynamic speakers in America today. More than 17,000 audiences in over 100 countries have attended his Schools of Wisdom and Conferences. Hundreds of invitations come to him from churches, colleges and business corporations. He is a noted author of over 250 books, including the best sellers, ***The Leadership Secrets of Jesus, Secrets of the Richest Man Who Ever Lived*** and the creator of ***The Master 7 Mentorship Program.*** Thousands view his weekly television program, ***Wisdom Keys with Mike Murdock.*** Many attend his Schools of Wisdom that he hosts in major cities...and his church, The Wisdom Center located at 4051 Denton Highway, Fort Worth, TX 76117.

The Wisdom Center • 1-817-759-BOOK • 1-817-759-0300
4051 Denton Highway • Fort Worth, Texas 76117

You Will Love Our Website...!

B-127/$7.00

ISBN 1-56394-133-3